In the Hoofsteps of Emooly

of Emooly

The Right for Boys and Girls to Be Treated as Equals

Written by Dustin Milligan • Illustrated by Meredith Luce

DC Canada Education Publishing

Written by: Dustin Milligan

Illustrated by: Meredith Luce

Editors: Leonard Judge, Debbie Gervais

Copy Editor: Anja Pujic

Cover Design: Meredith Luce

Published in 2013 by: DC Canada Education Publishing

130 Slater Street, Suite 960
Ottawa, On, Canada K1P 6E2
www.dc-canada.ca

· ·

**We acknowledge the financial support of the Government of Canada
through the Canada Book Fund for our publishing activities.**

In the Hoofsteps of Emooly Murphy

ISBN: 978-1-926776-51-4

· ·

Library and Archives Canada Cataloguing in Publication
Milligan, Dustin, 1984-
In the hoofsteps of Emooly Murphy : the right for boys and girls
to be treated as equals / by Dustin Milligan ; illustrated by Meredith Luce.
(The Charter for children)
ISBN 978-1-926776-52-1 (bound).--ISBN 978-1-926776-51-4 (pbk.)
1. Sex discrimination--Law and legislation--Canada--Juvenile literature.
I. Luce, Meredith, 1988- II. Title. III. Series: Charter for children
KE4399.M55 2013   j323.340971   C2012-905515-8
KF4483.C57M55 2013

Preface

The idea for *The Charter for Children* first emerged when I was a student at the Faculty of Law at McGill University. After my first year of studies, I was concerned that the common citizen wasn't equipped to understand our country's complicated legal system—one that I myself had only begun to comprehend. Children are at a further disadvantage in this regard, as they have limited capacity, strength and knowledge of their rights. Combining these concerns with my love for literature and the law, I took on this large project—writing a series of books that offer children a basic understanding of the *Canadian Charter of Rights and Freedoms*.

I would like to thank the Faculty of Law of McGill University, and most notably, Professor Shauna Van Praagh, who provided guidance during the course of much of this project and without whom the project would not have been possible. I would also like to thank those who have contributed their thoughts, insights, encouragement, time and puns—most notably, my three friends, Dorian Needham, Malcolm Dort and Josie Marks; Danielle Downing, Cecilie Rosairus and the students at King George Public School; Megan Howatt; Anton Suphal; Gregory Ko; Faizel Gulamhussein; Jessica Duarte; Christopher Ellis; the wonderful team at DC Canada Education Publishing; and my incredible family, Keith, Deborah, Olivia, Christian, Jolene and Shawn.

This series is dedicated to the children of Canada—may your voices be heard and considered, and may your childhoods be filled with respect and dignity.

Dustin Milligan

In a time not so long ago, at the Stampede in Calgary, Alberta, there lived a young cow named Eva.

One Saturday afternoon, as she ate her cowtton candy, Eva went to find her mother.

As Eva passed the front gates, an old bull yelled:

> *Take a ride on a cow! Take a ride on a bull!*
> *Eat cowtton candy until your belly is full!*
> *Welcome to Cow Town, where our cattle gave birth,*
> *To the latest and greatest outdoor show on earth!*

Eva's mother worked in cow riding. With her hoof on the fence, Eva watched her mother giving a ride to a young girl.

Eva's mother had a degree from Stampede School. It was the best cowllege in the country.

After getting their degrees, many cows worked in cow riding. All day long, they gave rides to children.

That's what Eva's mother did every day from nine to five.

Eva continued trotting through the Stampede grounds. As she finished her cowtton candy, she stopped to watch the bull riding.

Most of the bulls at the Stampede worked in bull riding. Unlike the cows, they jumped up and down all day long trying to get adults off their backs!

Eva watched as Mr. Bulldozer, the biggest and meanest bull at the Stampede, threw a man off his back.

As Eva licked the cowtton candy off her hooves, she saw the
Bulldozer twins out of the corner of her eye. The twins went to the
Grassy Junior High—the same school that Eva attended.

The Bulldozer twins were the meanest calves at school. They
constantly teased Eva about being poor.

Eva wanted to run and hide. She tried to avoid them, but it was
too late—the twins had already seen her.

The twins' father was Mr. Bulldozer. He made lots more moonies working in bull riding than Eva's mother made working in cow riding. And so he always bought the twins the latest fashions.

As they approached, the first twin mooed:

> *How do you like our new MooMoo Lemon t-shirts?*

And the second twin mooed:

> *They're cooler than your rags that are covered in dirt!*

Eva was too embarrassed to respond. Angry and ashamed, she trotted away with her head hung low.

The Bulldozer twins came from a family with lots of moonies. One evening, Eva had trotted by the Bulldozer's family home. The stall was as large as a two-car garage.

Eva had looked through the shiny bars. The family was watching the Canadian Country Music Awards on a big screen television.

She remembered hearing the hit song *Bull! I Feel Like a Cow!* and thinking about how unfair it all seemed.

She and her mother didn't own a television. They lived in a small rundown stall. The bars were rusty and the roof leaked.

Eva was tired of the Bulldozer twins teasing her about being poor.

And so, that evening, in their small rundown stall, Eva asked her mother for a new MooMoo Lemon shirt.

She mooed:

> *The calves at school have new boots and shirts,*
> *MooMoo Lemon, Moots, and brand name skirts!*
> *I know we don't have many moonies to spare,*
> *But I'm tired of being teased, it's just not fair!*

Eva's mother's hooves were sore from working all day at the Stampede. But even with all that hard work, she still couldn't afford new clothes.

Eva's mother felt ashamed that she didn't have enough moonies for her daughter. As she prepared their straw beds for the night, she looked her daughter in the eyes and mooed:

> *Darling dearest, it's time you were aware,*
> *For many years we've been treated unfair.*
> *I'll tell you a story beneath these stars,*
> *Then you'll know why we have rusted bars.*

As they lay down together beneath their leaky roof, her mother told her a story about City Stall and about how the cows had been treated poorly for many years.

Years ago, the bulls had nailed a sign to the front of City Stall.

It said: "Only Cattle Are Allowed Inside!"

The bulls had argued that the word "cattle" did not include cows. So cows weren't allowed inside City Stall. Only bulls could enter. Many called it the "Old Bulls' Club."

Eva's mother mooed:

> *I know that this sounds so very absurd.*
> *But I swear on my spots that it occurred!*

Then her mother told her about a group of brave cows that mooed up.

It was not fair that only bulls could enter City Stall. It was not fair that only bulls could make important decisions for the Stampede.

Eva's mother told her:

Emooly Murphy and four other cows from the prairies,
Argued with the bulls from the depths of their dairies.
They demanded that cows be allowed inside,
And mooed up to the bulls with all of their pride!

Emooly Murphy argued all the way to the highest court at the Stampede, the Privy Cowncil.

After a long debate, the Privy Cowncil mooed:

> It's clear the term "cattle" includes a cow,
> Cows are allowed inside City Stall now!

Thanks to Emooly Murphy and her four friends, cows could finally enter City Stall. At last, they could help make important decisions for the Stampede.

But the struggle continued even after cows were finally allowed inside City Stall.

There were still more bulls than cows in City Stall. So the cows had to moo extra loud to be heard!

The cows mooed for protection from bullies who didn't respect them.

They mooed for the right to stay home from work when their calves needed them.

Eva's mother finished her story by mooing:

Even after all of these years and tears,
The Stall is still full of bulls and steers!
It's the bulls and City Stall that decide,
To pay cows so little for cattle rides!

Eva learned that City Stall paid bulls more moonies than cows at the Stampede.

As she lay her head in the straw, Eva dreamed about Emooly Murphy and all of her courage. Emooly had mooed up to the bulls so that cows could be treated fairly at the Stampede.

But still, years later, cows were paid less moonies than bulls. They were still being treated unfairly.

Both cow riding and bull riding required the same degrees from cowllege. Both jobs were very important to the Stampede.

Eva wanted to follow in the hoofsteps of Emooly Murphy. She wanted to help her mother and stand up for the cows at the Stampede.

The next morning, Eva told her mom:

You must not go to work today!
You must protest your unfair pay!
You and the cows must go on strike,
Until cows and bulls are paid alike!

Eva's mother looked into her daughter's big brown eyes and picked up the phone.

She mooed:

> *We must not go to work today!*
> *We must protest our unfair pay!*
> *We cows must go on strike,*
> *Until cows and bulls are paid alike.*

Before they finished breakfast that morning, Eva and her mother had phoned every cow at the Stampede.

That day, not one cow went to work. The cows agreed that they would not work until they received the same pay as the bulls.

And that day, the Stampede was in a panic.

Without the cows, the Stampede couldn't offer cow rides. And with no cow rides, many children started to cry.

The next day, the cows organized a protest outside of City Stall. Eva and her mother led the cows around in a circle.

A reporter from the *Calgary Herald* asked Eva what was going on.

Eva mooed:

> *My mother works as hard as any bull,*
> *With the same degree from Stampede School!*
> *She is needed for the Stampede's success,*
> *But in terms of moonies, she makes much less!*

Since there were no cow rides, children no longer wanted to go the Stampede. The Stampede grounds were empty.

Even some bulls were forced to close down their stalls. They were going out of business.

Mr. Bulldozer was furious! It was an emergency.

He mooed:

> *All cattle in Calgary hear my call!*
> *We must meet tonight at City Stall!*

That night, City Stall held an emergency meeting. The bulls and cows needed to work together or else the Stampede would go out of business.

The cows and bulls mooed for hours and hours. The cows demanded that they make the same amount of moonies as the bulls.

Though there were many different opinions, all cows and bulls were given a chance to moo their concerns.

Even so, Eva was worried. There were still more bulls than cows at City Stall.

What would they decide?

After many hours of mooing, and just before dawn, City Stall finally came to an agreement.

Even Mr. Bulldozer agreed that cows must be paid fairly.

Mr. Bulldozer mooed:

My fellow cattle, there's no reason to despair.
We will raise cows' pay and do what's fair!
Bulls and cows must be treated with respect.
And every law at the Stall must reflect,
Fairness for all cattle at the Stampede.
Only then will the Stampede succeed!

Finally, the cows and bulls would be paid the same at the Stampede.

Eva hugged her mother.

As the sun rose the next morning, the cattle returned to work. And just like before, the cows were busy giving cow rides to children.

Eva was proud of her mother. She had raised her moo and was now making the same amount of moonies as a bull.

As the twins passed her by, Eva kicked her hooves, waving her tail proudly in the air. She didn't need a MooMoo Lemon t-shirt to make her feel important. She was no longer afraid.

And that night, after a long day at the Stampede, Eva and her mother came home to their stall.

With the extra moonies her mother was now making, they had gotten their leaky roof fixed. As they lay down on the warm dry straw, they felt proud that they were finally being treated fairly by City Stall.

Before turning out the light, Eva mooed to her mother:

It feels much better to lie down in the straw,
Knowing we're being treated fairly under the law.
Like Emooly Murphy, we put up a good fight.
One more hoofstep for cows and now good night!

Note for Parents and Teachers:

This story seeks to teach children about the right to equal treatment and freedom from discrimination on the basis of sex, which is guaranteed by section 15(1) of the *Canadian Charter of Rights and Freedoms*. This section provides that:

> *Every individual is equal before and under the law and has the right to the equal protection and equal benefit of the law without discrimination and, in particular, without discrimination based on...sex.*[1]

Although this provision guarantees equal treatment to a number of groups, this story focuses on the struggle of women to gain equality with men since they have been the primary targets of discrimination based on sex.

To highlight this historic struggle, the story centres around City Stall—the political body at the Stampede. The story of the cows' exclusion from City Stall is an analogy to women's historic exclusion from the Canadian Senate. Prior to 1929, women were excluded from being appointed as senators. Emily Murphy, Irene Parlby, Nellie McClung, Louise McKinney, and Henrietta Edwards, who later became known as the "Famous Five," petitioned the Supreme Court of Canada to rule on whether the term "qualified persons" in the constitution included women, and therefore, whether women could be appointed to the Senate. On appeal to the British Judicial Committee of the Privy Council, it held that the term "persons" included women as well as men, allowing women to be appointed to the Senate, or in reference to this story, allowing cows to enter City Stall.[2]

The struggle for fair treatment continued even after cows received the right to be members of City Stall. This is similar to the ongoing struggle of Canadian women in the battle for equality. Although women received full rights to political office early in the 20th century, Canadian political bodies have been, and still are, dominated by men. For example, women have never held more than a quarter of the seats in the House of Commons although they account for more than half of the Canadian population.[3] Women have therefore remained under-represented during discussions on many important issues ranging from domestic abuse, to maternity leave, to pay equity—the central theme of this story.

Pay equity is the idea that women and men should be paid the same amount for work of equal or comparable value. Even today, jobs that have been historically perceived as "women's jobs" are chronically underpaid and women continue to be economically disadvantaged in the workforce.[4] For example, according to Statistics Canada, women working full time in 2008 earned only 71.4% as much as their male counterparts.[5]

In this story, City Stall pays less to cattle for cow riding than bull riding even though the work is of equal or comparable value. This low pay places Eva and her mother in a position of poverty and affects their dignity and self-worth. The cows therefore decide to go on strike until City Stall provides pay equity for the cows.

This story provides a brief analogy of the historic struggle for women's rights in this country, and more broadly, of the struggle for greater equality based on sex. By the end of the story, when City Stall raises the pay for cow riding, it is in the context of this long struggle. It is a struggle of many "hoofsteps," with many cows (and even some bulls) leading the march, each one approaching a greater and richer sense of equality.

[1] *Canadian Charter of Rights and Freedoms*, s 15(1), Part I of the *Constitution Act*, 1982, being Schedule B to the *Canada Act* 1982 (UK), 1982, c 11.

[2] *Edwards v Canada* (Attorney General), [1930] AC 124, 1929 UKPC 86.

[3] Meagan Fitzpatrick, "Record Number of Women Elected" CBC News (3 May 2011), online: CBC News Online <http://www.cbc.ca/news/politics/canadavotes2011/story/2011/05/03/cv-election-women.html>.

[4] *Newfoundland (Treasury Board) v NAPE*, [2004] 3 SCR 381, 24 DLR (4th) 294.

[5] Julie Cool, *Wage Gap Between Men and Women*, Library of Parliament Research Publications (29 July 2010), online: Parliament of Canada <http://www.parl.gc.ca/Content/LOP/ResearchPublications/2010-30-e.htm#a4>.

Questions for children:

1. Why do the Bulldozer twins bully Eva? Why is Eva's family poorer than the Bulldozer's family? Is it fair?

2. What is City Stall? Why is it important that cows are heard and represented in City Stall?

3. Why do Eva and her mother go on strike? Why does City Stall decide to pay cows more moonies?

4. What can you do to make sure that girls and boys are treated as equals in your school and your community?